Roxa and the Fairy Godbrother

Meg Harper

Illustrated by Clare Elsom

Contents

OXFORD
UNIVERSITY PRESS

The Broken Wand

Roxanne hated her hair. It was too short and too curly.

'I wish I had long, straight hair,' she said.

Flash! Bang!

A fairy with huge, pointy ears crash-landed on Roxanne's toy farm.

'Oops!' he said. 'I've broken my wand.'

'Never mind your wand,' said Roxanne crossly. 'Look what you've done to my farm! Who are you, anyway?'

'I'm Dazz,' said the fairy proudly. 'I'm your fairy godbrother.'

'My fairy god*brother*?' said Roxanne.
'Aren't you supposed to be a girl?'

'No,' said Dazz. 'There are new rules.'

'Hmm,' said Roxanne. 'You've wrecked
my toy farm, you've broken your wand,
and you're not even sparkly. Can you do
any spells?'

'Not without my wand,' said Dazz.

'Ta-dah!' Roxanne gave Dazz her toothbrush.

'Use that instead!' she said. 'I want long, straight hair, please.'

Dazz waved the toothbrush. It blew up in a puff of minty stars.

'Yes!' Dazz cheered.

Roxanne stared at her hair in horror. It was very long and very straight ... but it was also white and spiky. Toothbrush hair!

'Do something!' Roxanne cried. 'Quickly!'

'But my wand is broken!' said Dazz, panicking.

'What's that behind your ear?' said
Roxanne.

'Of course!' said Dazz. 'It's my spare
wand!'

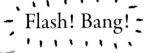

Roxanne's toothbrush hair
disappeared.

'Sorry,' said Dazz. 'Shall I try again?'

'No thanks,' said Roxanne. 'I've decided I like my curls.'

'OK,' said Dazz. 'Shall I fix your farm instead?'

'Noooo!' shrieked Roxanne, but it was too late.

'Oops!' said Dazz.

I Want a Fairy Godmother!

Roxanne was getting ready for bed.

'Why do I have to have a fairy god*brother*?' she grumbled to her cat, Tiggy. 'Why can't I be like Cinderella?'

She stomped into her bedroom.

'Ta-dah!' said Dazz, grinning. 'Your wish is my command! Meet Flora and Dora.'

Roxanne stared in horror. Two strange girls were having a pillow fight on her bed!

'*I'm* going to marry Prince Charming!' shouted Flora, the stroppy girl. She bashed Dora round the head.

'No, *I* am!' yelled Dora, the grotty girl. She whacked Flora in the chest.

Oh no, thought Roxanne. *Dazz heard my wish about being like Cinderella.*

'I didn't mean I want ugly sisters!' she cried. 'I want a fairy god*mother*!'

'Oops!' said Dazz. 'Sorry!'

'Get rid of them,' said Roxanne. 'Before my mum hears!'

'I don't know if I can,' said Dazz, looking worried.

'Well, try!' hissed Roxanne. 'Quickly!'

Dazz took out his wand. He screwed up his eyes.

Flash! Bang!

'Ta-dah!' he said.

The ugly sisters vanished and two chimpanzees appeared! One was climbing the curtains. The other was swinging from the lampshade.

'Oops!' said Dazz.

'Do something!' shrieked Roxanne. 'Fast!'

Flash! Bang!

'Ta-dah!' said Dazz. The chimpanzees were gone – but two crazy puppies were fighting on the bed!

'Oops!' said Dazz.

'Try again, *please*!' begged Roxanne.
'I can hear Mum coming upstairs!'

Flash! Bang!

'Ta-dah!' said Dazz.

No puppies. No girls. Nothing at all.

'Phew!' said Dazz.

'Thank goodness,' sighed Roxanne.
'Time for bed at last.'

She turned back her duvet.

'Aaagh!' screamed Roxanne.

'Oops!' said Dazz.

Fairy Dust

Roxanne was having a bad dream. She
dreamed she was in the desert and there
was a massive sandstorm.

She woke up coughing and looked
around. Her bedroom was covered in sand!

'Dazz!' she hissed. 'What have you
done?'

Flash! Bang!

'Oops!' said Dazz. 'Sorry. I was trying to make fairy dust.'

'Well, it didn't work,' said Roxanne.

'Shall I try again?' asked Dazz.

'I'm not sure ... ' said Roxanne nervously.

Flash! Bang!

'Achoo!' sneezed Roxanne. 'Achoo! Achoo! Achoo!' She sneezed so hard that she blew Dazz right across the room!

Dazz waved his wand.

'Oops! That must have been sneezing powder,' Dazz gasped. 'I'd better try again.'

'Dazz, I don't think ... ' started Roxanne. But it was too late.

Flash! Bang!

Scratch, scratch, scratch! Now
Roxanne itched all over. It was itchier than
chickenpox!

'Do something, Dazz,' Roxanne begged.
'That must have been itching powder!'

'I don't know what to do!' cried Dazz.

'Do anything!'
shouted Roxanne.
'Just stop me
itching!'

'Urgh!' spluttered Roxanne.

She had stopped itching. But now she was sitting in the pond in the garden!

Roxanne was covered in slime. So was her cat, Tiggy.

'Just wait till I get hold of you, Dazz,' Roxanne growled.

She stomped upstairs and flung open
her bedroom door.

'Wow!' gasped Roxanne.

'It's fairy dust,' said Dazz, smugly. 'Who
says I'm not as good as a fairy god*mother*?'
'I do,' said Roxanne.

About the author

I'm not just an author – I also direct an award-winning youth theatre, teach creative writing, run museum workshops and even work as a school counsellor! My books have been shortlisted for several awards and right now I'm getting into storytelling too – my stories are the 'all join in!' sort, so do invite me to your school! In my spare time, I swim, walk, run and, of course, read. I adore trips out for tea and cake – which is why I need so much exercise.

I really enjoyed writing this book because Dazz and Roxanne have been kicking around my head for ages – I love playing about with fairy tales! I hope it makes you giggle – I love laughing myself.